Color & Light

▲ David Evans and Claudette Williams ◻

DORLING KINDERSLEY
LONDON • NEW YORK • STUTTGART

A DORLING KINDERSLEY BOOK

Project Editor Stella Love
Art Editor Nicki Simmonds
Managing Editor Jane Yorke
Managing Art Editor Chris Scollen
Production Jayne Wood
Photography by Daniel Pangbourne
U.S. Editor B. Alison Weir

First American Edition, 1993
2 4 6 8 10 9 7 5 3 1

Published in the United States by
Dorling Kindersley, Inc., 232 Madison Avenue
New York, New York 10016

Library of Congress Cataloguing-in-Publication Data

Evans, David. 1937 -
  Color and light / by David Evans and Claudette Williams.--1st American ed.
    p. cm.--(Let's explore science)
  Includes index.
  Summary : Uses simple observations and experiments to explore the properties of
color and light.
  ISBN 1-56458-207-8
  1. Color--Juvenile literature. 2. Color --Experiments--Juvenile literature.
3. Light--Juvenile literature. 4. Light--Experiments--Juvenile literature.
[1. Color--Experiments. 2. Light--Experiments. 3. Experiments.]
1. Williams. Claudette. II. Title. III. Series.
QC495.5. E93 1993
536.6–dc20   92-53480
                                                      CIP
                                                      AC

Reproduced by J. Film Process Singapore Pte., Ltd.
Printed and bound in Belgium by Proost

Dorling Kindersley would like to thank the following for their help
in producing this book: Susanna Price (for additional photography);
Coral Mula (for safety symbol artwork); Mark Richards (for jacket design);
the Franklin Delano Roosevelt School, London; Berol Limited, King's Lynn.
Dorling Kindersley would also like to give special thanks to the following for
appearing in this book: Natalie Agada; Sammy Arias; Hannah Capleton;
Gregory Coleman; Luca Hayward; Foyzul Kadir; Max Lee; Tony Locke;
Rachael Malicki; Charlie McCarthy; Kim Ng; Tanya Pham; Daniel Sach;
Anthony Singh; Milo Taylor.

Contents

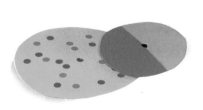

Note to parents and teachers

Young children are forever asking questions about the things they see, touch, hear, smell, and taste. The **Let's Explore Science** series aims to foster children's natural curiosity and encourages them to use their senses to find out about science. Each book features a variety of experiments based on one topic, which draw on a young child's everyday experiences. By investigating familiar activities, such as bouncing a ball, making cakes, or clapping hands, young children will learn that science plays an important part in the world around them.

Investigative approach

Young children can only begin to understand science if they are stimulated to think and to find out for themselves. For these reasons, an open-ended questioning approach is used in the **Let's Explore Science** books and, wherever possible, results of experiments are not shown. Children are encouraged to make their own scientific discoveries and to interpret them according to their own ideas. This investigative approach to learning makes science exciting and not just about acquiring "facts." This way of learning will assist children in many areas of their education.

Using the books

Before starting an experiment, check the text and pictures to ensure that you have gathered all necessary equipment. Allow children to help in this process and to suggest materials to use. Once ready, it is important to let children decide how to carry out the experiment and what the result means to them. You can help by asking questions, such as, "What do you think will happen?" or "What did you do?"

Household equipment

All the experiments can be carried out easily at home. In most cases, inexpensive household objects and materials are used.

Guide to experiments

The *Guide to experiments* on pages 28-29 is intended to help parents, teachers, or helpers using this book with children. It gives an outline of the scientific principles underlying the experiments, includes useful tips for carrying out the activities, suggests alternative equipment to use, and additional activities to try.

Safe experimenting

This symbol appears next to experiments where children may require adult supervision or assistance, for example, when they are heating things or using sharp tools.

About this book

Color and Light encourages young children to investigate the concepts of light and dark, shadow and reflection, the color spectrum, and camouflage. Children are challenged to create shadows and reflections and to mix and match colors. The experiments enable children to discover that:

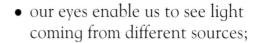

- our eyes enable us to see light coming from different sources;
- we see objects because they give out, or reflect light;
- light can be seen through some materials to varying degrees, while other materials stop light and absorb the rays;
- shining light onto shiny surfaces produces reflections;
- when light is shone through transparent objects the direction of light is sometimes changed;
- if a beam of light is interrupted, a shadow may form, the position and size of which is predictable;
- when a light ray is bent by a prism, it is split into a spectrum of colors, which always appear in the same order;
- we see color because materials absorb or reflect the different colors in light to varying degrees.

With your help, young children will enjoy exploring the world of science and discover that finding out is fun.

David Evans and Claudette Williams

What can you see?

Is it easy to do things with one eye closed?
What can you see in the dark?

With one eye closed
Can you close one eye
and touch your nose?
Can you do the same
thing with your other
eye closed?

With a light on
Close your eyes and cover them.
Can you tell when a flashlight is
on? What happens when you bring
the flashlight nearer?

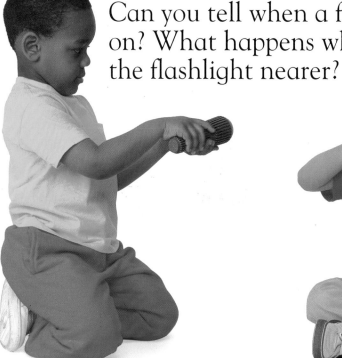

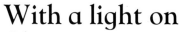

With two eyes covered
Cover your eyes. What
colors do you see?

In a hiding place
Ask some friends
to help you make a
hiding place with a
blanket and some
chairs or boxes.
Can you make
it really dark
inside?

Sit inside your hiding place.
What can you see in the
dark? Can you think of ways
to make it light inside your
hiding place?

Can you see through it?

What happens when you shine
a flashlight on things?

Light on things
Gather lots of different objects.
Can you find things made of
wood, fabric, metal, plastic,
china, and paper? What do
you see when you shine
a flashlight on them?

Which things
are shiny?
Which things
are dull?

Light under your hand
Can you see light through your hand?

Light through things
Shine your flashlight close to things. What kinds of objects does the light shine through?

Seeing through things
What do you see when you look through a sheet of colored plastic?

13

Can you make shadows?

Look at shadows indoors and outdoors.

Never look directly at the sun.

Finding shadows
Can you find your shadow on a sunny day? Is it always the same shape and size?

Catching shadows
Can you catch a friend's shadow?

Making shadows
Which things make a shadow?

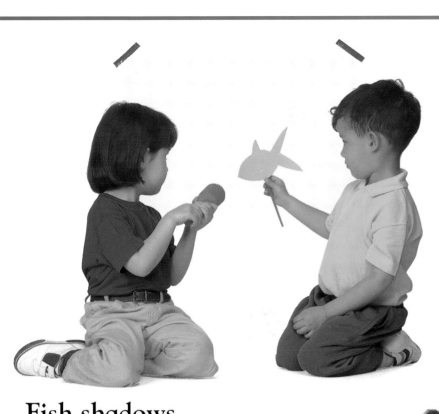

Hand shadows
Can you make the shadow of a dog's head? Can you make a butterfly?

Fish shadows
Cut out a paper fish. Tape a drinking straw to the fish to make a handle. Can you make fish shadows swim across the wall?

Face shadows
Ask a friend to make a face shadow. Can you put a sheet of paper on the wall and draw around the shadow of your friend's face?

Can you see yourself?

What do you see when you look at something shiny?

Shiny objects
What shiny things can you find? What do you see when you look closely at them?

Bendable mirror
Look into a flexible plastic mirror. How can you make your face look long and thin?

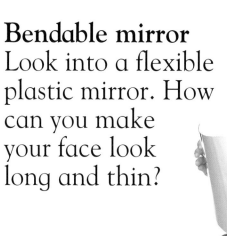

Bowl of water
What do you see in a bowl of water? What will happen if you put your finger in the water?

Two mirrors
Can you use
two mirrors to
see the back of
your head?

One mirror
Can you look into
a mirror and touch
your nose?

Mirror picture
Can you draw or
trace a picture
while looking in
a mirror?

What can mirrors do?

Try these experiments with mirrors and a magnifying glass to see what happens.

Make a periscope
Fix two small mirrors to a garden stake with lumps of modeling clay.

Can you use your periscope to see over a high wall?

Can you see around a corner?

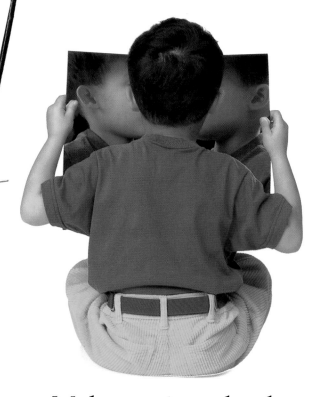

Make a mirror book
Stick two plastic mirrors together with tape so that they make a book. What do you see when you slowly fold the mirrors together?

Make light change
What happens to
a light beam when
you shine it through
a magnifying glass
onto a wall?

Make light turn corners
Shine a flashlight onto a
mirror through a tube.
Can you catch the
light in another tube
and make it turn
a corner?

**Make light
bounce**
Can you make
light bounce onto
the ceiling with
a small mirror?

19

Can you see a rainbow?

Try these experiments and see what can happen to light. Can you see lots of colors?

Mirror, flashlight, and water
Fill a shallow plastic tray with water. Ask a friend to hold a mirror in the water.

Prism
What can you see when you look through a prism?

Shine a flashlight on the bottom of the mirror, through the water. Hold up a piece of white paper to catch the rainbow.

What colors do you see?

Bubbles
Can you see more colors in bubbles when you are indoors or outside?

Water and oil
Put a bowl of water in sunlight. Put some drops of machine oil in the water. What do you see?

Colored lights
Cover one flashlight with blue cellophane and one flashlight with red. Shine both flashlights onto the same spot in a white box.

Which color do you think you will see?

Which colors do you see?

Can you sort things by color?
Can you make colors change?

Sorting colors

Collect lots of different things.
Can you sort them into groups
by color? What do the colors
look like when you wear

sunglasses? What happens to the
colors when you look at them
through a sheet of colored
plastic?

Spinning colors

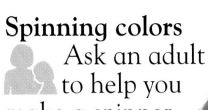 Ask an adult to help you make a spinner. Cut a circle out of card. Decorate it with a painted pattern or colored stickers.

Make a hole in the center of the circle. Push a crayon through the hole. What will happen to the pattern when you spin the spinner?

Mixing colors

Add drops of food coloring to a jar of water. What colors can you make by mixing some food colorings? Make a guess before you try.

Can you make colors?

How many different colors can you make and use?

Light and dark colors
How many shades of red can you make with paint?

What will happen when you add black or white paint to red paint? Does adding water change the color?

Mixing colors
How many shades of green can you mix with your paints?

Different colors
Can you paint a picture using lots of colors?

Looking at colors

Cut coffee filters into strips. Put a blob of ink on one end of a strip with a marker. Hold the paper so that it just dips into some water. What do you think will happen?

Now balance a circle of filter paper on a paper cup. Put a spot of food coloring on the paper and slowly drip a few drops of water on it. What happens?

Try using a different color. Will the same thing happen?

Can you hide or match it?

Can you use paint or colors
to hide things?

Hiding your hand
Put your hand on
some striped paper.
Can you hide your
hand against the
paper with paint?

Which colors
show up best
from far away?
Which colors
do not show up
very well?

Seeing colors
Ask a friend to stand
far away from you and
to hold up a picture.

Matching skin color

Draw around your hand and then color it in. Which colors will you use to match your skin?

Animal camouflage

Cut out some paper animals. Can you make or paint a background scene in which to hide them?

Matching hair and eye color

Make a picture of a friend. Can you match the color of your friend's hair and eyes?

Index

Guide to experiments

The notes below briefly outline the scientific principles underlying the experiments and include suggestions for alternative equipment to use and activities to try.

What can you see? 10-11

Children explore the concept of light and dark and discover that light is necessary to see. Other activities that children can try include doing a simple task in light and then dark conditions, and finding their way around a room with their eyes closed or blindfolded. You could also ask children questions, such as, "Where can you find light?"

Can you see through it? 12-13

These activities demonstrate to children that materials are transparent (let light through), translucent (let some light through), or opaque (stop light). Another activity for children to try is shining a flashlight through, and looking through, a variety of liquids then describing what they see.

Can you make shadows? 14-15

Children discover that a shadow forms when they stand between the sun, or light source, and a light-colored surface. By experimenting with flashlights, children see that the shape and size of a shadow depend on how far the object is from the light source.

Can you see yourself? 16-17

Experiments with mirrors and shiny objects help children understand the laws of reflection. By using flexible mirrors and other rounded, shiny objects, children can explore how the image reflected from a curved surface will be distorted.

What can mirrors do? 18-19

By making a periscope, children explore practical ways in which reflection can be used. The mirror book introduces the concept of multiple images. The magnifier activity can be extended by asking children to shine light through other lenses, such as eyeglasses and clear bottles of water.

Can you see a rainbow? 20-21

Children investigate how white light can be separated into a rainbow when it is refracted as it passes through a prism, a soap bubble, or oil on the surface of water. They will also discover how shining red and blue lights together will produce magenta light.

Which colors do you see? 22-23

By using colored filters and sunglasses, children see the results of absorption, transmission, and reflection of colored light. Cellophane candy wrappers can be used as colored filters. Spinning multicolored spinners and mixing food dyes demonstrate how colors mix to produce other colors.

Can you make colors? 24-25

Experiments to mix and dilute paints give children an appreciation of the vast range of colors that exist. By carrying out the chromatography experiments, children can see which colors have been used to create a colored ink or pigment. Blotting paper can be used instead of coffee filter paper.

Can you hide or match it? 26-27

These experiments introduce ideas about camouflage. Children find out which colors show up best from a distance and then consider the ways animals use color to camouflage and protect themselves. Children can extend their exploration of camouflage by thinking of ways to hide themselves in outdoor locations, such as in a meadow or on a beach.